First World War
and Army of Occupation
War Diary
France, Belgium and Germany

16 DIVISION
49 Infantry Brigade
Prince Albert's (Somerset Light Infantry)
6th Battalion
1 March 1918 - 30 April 1919

WO95/1979/4

The Naval & Military Press Ltd
www.nmarchive.com
Published in association with The National Archives

Published by

The Naval & Military Press Ltd

Unit 10 Ridgewood Industrial Park,

Uckfield, East Sussex,

TN22 5QE England

Tel: +44 (0) 1825 749494

www.naval-military-press.com

www.nmarchive.com

This diary has been reprinted in facsimile from the original. Any imperfections are inevitably reproduced and the quality may fall short of modern type and cartographic standards.

© **Crown Copyright**
Images reproduced by permission of The National Archives, London, England, 2015.

Contents

Document type	Place/Title	Date From	Date To
Heading	1979/4 6 Battalion Somerset Light Infantry June 1918-Apr 1919		
Heading	16th Division 49th Infy Bde. 6th Bn Somerset Lt Infy Jun 1918-Apl 1919 From 43 Bde 14 Div		
War Diary	Sains Les Fressin	01/06/1918	18/06/1918
War Diary	Boulogne	01/08/1918	01/08/1918
War Diary	Hubersent	02/08/1918	19/08/1918
War Diary	Dieval Noeux Les Mines	20/08/1918	20/08/1918
War Diary	Mines	21/08/1918	22/08/1918
War Diary	Cambrin	22/08/1918	31/08/1918
Heading	6th Somerset Light Infantry Volume 40 War Diary For September 1918		
War Diary	Cambrin	01/09/1918	08/09/1918
War Diary	In The Line	09/09/1918	12/09/1918
War Diary	Auchy	13/09/1918	13/09/1918
War Diary	Cambrin	14/09/1918	21/09/1918
War Diary	Braddell Point	22/09/1918	23/09/1918
War Diary	Auchy	24/09/1918	27/09/1918
War Diary	Drouvin	27/09/1918	30/09/1918
Heading	Volume 40. War Diary. 6th Service Battalion Somerset Light Infantry for the month of October 1918		
War Diary	Drouvin	01/10/1918	02/10/1918
War Diary	Sailly La Bourse	03/10/1918	07/10/1918
War Diary	Noeux Les. Mines	08/10/1918	17/10/1918
War Diary	Cambrin Berclau	18/10/1918	18/10/1918
War Diary	Annoeulin Pont A Mari	19/10/1918	19/10/1918
War Diary	Bachy	20/10/1918	20/10/1918
War Diary	Rumes	21/10/1918	24/10/1918
War Diary	In The Line	25/10/1918	28/10/1918
War Diary	Tantignies	29/10/1918	31/10/1918
Heading	War Diary 6th Bn. Somerset L.I. for November 1918 Volume No. 41		
War Diary	Tantignies	01/11/1918	06/11/1918
War Diary	Rumes	07/11/1918	10/11/1918
War Diary	Bruyelles	11/11/1918	14/11/1918
War Diary	Rumes	15/11/1918	15/11/1918
War Diary	Bersee	16/11/1918	30/11/1918
War Diary	War Diary For December 1918 Volume No. 42 6th Bn. Somerset L.I.		
War Diary	Bersee	01/12/1918	31/12/1918
Heading	Volume 43 War Diary 6th Battalion Somerset Light Infantry January 1919		
War Diary	Bersee	01/01/1919	31/01/1919
Heading	Volume 44. War Diary for Month of February 1919. 6th Battalion Somerset Light Infantry Bef.		
War Diary	Bersee	01/02/1919	28/02/1919
Heading	War Diary Volume 45 of 6th Service Battalion Somerset Light Infantry for the month of March 1919		
War Diary	Bersee	01/03/1918	31/03/1918

Heading	War Diary For Month of April 1919. Volume No. 46. 6th Service Battalion Somerset Light Infantry Vol		
War Diary	Bersee Bef France	01/04/1919	30/04/1919

1979/4

6 Battalion Somerset Light Infantry.

June 1916 – Apr 1919

16TH DIVISION
49TH INFY BDE

6TH BN SOMERSET LT INFY

JUN 1918 - APL 1919

FROM. { 43 Bde
        14 DIV.

Jun "18
opl "19

49/10   6 Somerset L/   16 17

Army Form C. 2118.

WAR DIARY
or
INTELLIGENCE SUMMARY.
(Erase heading not required.)

Instructions regarding War Diaries and Intelligence Summaries are contained in F. S. Regs., Part II. and the Staff Manual respectively. Title pages will be prepared in manuscript.

452 35 Remarks and references to Appendices

39 N.
10 sheets

Place	Date	Hour	Summary of Events and Information	Remarks
	JUNE			
GINCHY FRESNOY	1	Fine	Baths at LEBIEZ	
	2	Fine	C of E service 10 AM	
	3	Fine	Equipment & Clothing inspection; Inoculation parade. Lt Col A.D. Bollard in command of Brigade Training Staffs in the absence of the B.G.C.	Brigade Diary? 200 m.c.
	4	Fine	Rest after inoculation	
	5	Fine	do	
	6	Fine	Parades PT-BF, sawing drill	
	7	Fine	Bath at LEBIEZ	
	8	Fine	Parades. Cups for appointed Inspection L' Blackburn H Kings x	
		10 the Kent	present. Bias on new percussion	
	9	Fine	Church Sunday	
	10	Fine	Parades. PT B.F. drill & Communicating Drill	
	11	Fine	Inspection of mules found fit for use at ROLLENCOURT	
	12	Fine	Inspection of learning rescued by B.G.C. & L/C of Bn, umpires, B	
			Lampal	
	13	Fine	Parades commencing at 16 awards Force 145	man and

Army Form C. 2118.

WAR DIARY
or
INTELLIGENCE SUMMARY.
(Erase heading not required.)

Instructions regarding War Diaries and Intelligence Summaries are contained in F.S. Regs., Part II. and the Staff Manual respectively. Title pages will be prepared in manuscript.

Place	Date	Hour	Summary of Events and Information	Remarks and references to Appendices
1918 June	14		Leaving personnel moved to TORCY. arrived in billets 3.10 pm	
	15		Sun. Parade Drill 95-10.7	
	16		Entrucy, advance & 6 curries at HESDIN 9 pm 17-6-18. transport to TARES by road	N.S.R. 9.31
			to 14 Div. Train St MARIE FARM 2 miles SW SQUIRE. Bn. transferred to the 16 Div	43 G.M. numbers 4
	17		Bn. marches to HESDIN entrained. transports unaccompanied arrived Folkestone	
			2 am. reached BOULOGNE 11 am.	
	18		Bn. entrained 3 pm arrived at FOLKESTONE, & entrained for ALDERSHOT. arrived	
			there 11 pm. marched to Bourley Camp were placed under Canvas.	

R. Crawford
Lt Col
16-7/9/18 18/9/18

N. Crawford
Capt y
6 Leicesters
6/7/18

WAR DIARY or INTELLIGENCE SUMMARY

6th Somerset L.I.

Army Form C. 2118

Place	Date	Hour	Summary of Events and Information	Remarks and references to Appendices
BOULOGNE	1918 Aug 1		The Bn embarked at FOLKESTONE on S.S. PRINCESS VICTORIA disembarked at BOULOGNE marched to OSTROHOVE REST. Stayed here the night, others arrived to various Opt 8.30 PM 2/8/18 & entraining through P.B. at 39 Officers & 140 Other Ranks (600 rations)	16 Div AA/Q 258/34 EG3 40/1/G. SS3 (revision) 32/M
HUBERSENT	2		Entrained BOULOGNE detrained SAMER marched to HUBERSENT joined Bn. Transport arrived in bivouacs 5pm. 1 Coy in billets LA POSSE FARM	
	3		Coy Parade. Inspections. Cleaning of billets.	
	4		Church Parade. The Commanding Officer had a Conference for Coy Commanders. Personnel for Div Coy class warned of 3pm	
	5		Storing Drill Parades. Section Training. P.B.T. Clearance over S.M. for N/Cpls. Full marching order P.B.T. inspection. Autumn Officers under the Commanding Officer drill. Lump hopping. Bayonet & trench firing classes	
			Bn Lewis Gun class overnised.	
	6		Div Drill & Musketry Classes RIDMORE and THOMAS Hornsey P.T. O.T. Officers P.B.T. class. Buglers & Sig section nevies Sniping classes. Reinforcement.	
			Receiving Capt M.S.W. Palmer, M.C. was a member of a court of Inquiry on bro G. Shelley at Aldersea. Captain D inquiry assembled at Bn from Freques vice bus G Shelley at Aldersea. President Capt G/8/Bn Capt. Walbian, Lieut H Cleff Lieut T.J. Hawkins	

WAR DIARY
or
INTELLIGENCE SUMMARY.
(Erase heading not required)

Army Form C. 2118.

Place	Date	Hour	Summary of Events and Information	Remarks and references to Appendices
HUBERSENT	Aug 7		Fine. Drill. Depts under S.M. Section training for the purpose of reorganising under P.B.S. Class for N.C.O's under S.M. First Class for Officers. Reconnoitered training. Night operations postponed. Gas Drill cr.	
	8		Wet. Platoon training. String of Trenches. P.D.T. Classes for Officers N.C.O's. Shicken Bearer Dg. Bomber and Scouts. Recreational Training.	
	9		Fine. Drill & D/Ops under S.M. 2 Coy. route march tactical exercise. 1 Coy on Bomb range. 1 Coy Coy Drill & attack. P.B.3. Lecture Scheme Recreational Training. Classes for Officers under P.T Instructors. Drill rank N.C.O's under S.M. Inspection of Transport by Major Latham WCK. A.S.C.	
	10		Fine. No 3 Coy on Bomb range. No 1,2 & 4 Coy Company Drill & Section Exercises. No 4 Coy. Loading Parade under S.M. Classes for Stricken Bearer, Snipers. Recreational Training. Two Drafts at 50 N.C.O. & men proceeded to Gas Course at XIII Corps. Gas School. ARMES - L/c- DUSAMS.	
	11		Fine. Church Parade Service. Medical Inspection of Men. Lectures on General Machine Guns. Reconnoitre Training.	

WAR DIARY or INTELLIGENCE SUMMARY

Army Form C. 2118.

Place	Date	Hour	Summary of Events and Information	Remarks and references to Appendices
HÉBUTERNE	12		Fine. Half Bn on A-B Ranges. 1 Coy on Br Ranges. No Coy Platoon Training. Scouting Drill under S.M. P.P.T. Branch discipline. Officers & N.C.O. Class P.P.T.	
	13		Bn entrained to #49 Inf/Bde. Recreational Training	
	14		Bn Br marched to the coast near STAPLES for bathing, arrived back in billets 9.15 p.m. Fine Coy drill. Lewis Learning. Lectures typ of equipment by off Bn. P.P.T. Night operations. 2 Classes for Bombers. Scouting under S.M. Officers P.P.T. Class under Eng W. Wky. Stretcher Bearer Class. Recreational Training	
	15		Inspection of MC Room by Capt. Sir H.S. Howe RCG RAMC. Guns mg by 1st Army. Fine. 1st & 2nd Coys on A-B Ranges. 3 Coy Platoon Training. 4 Coy digging. P.P.T. Classes for Officers & NCO's. 2/Lts under S.M. Bombing Classes. S.B's Ley Class. Recreational Training	
	16		Fine. Lecture demonstration of the Commanding Officer to all officers. Training of Platoon. Lecture on Bayonet fighting by 2/Lt Campbell S.A. Demonstrations of Spec: Wiring by 59 Coy R.E. Drill under O.C. Special Arms classes. Recreation & Training. Trumpeters sent from 49 Inf Bde. Bn, 18th December to 12 Lt Col. Geo 19 Coy Saluting drill under S.M. P.P.T.	NBB Form over 25 by fm

Army Form C. 2118.

WAR DIARY
or
INTELLIGENCE SUMMARY.
(Erase heading not required.)

Instructions regarding War Diaries and Intelligence Summaries are contained in F. S. Regs., Part II. and the Staff Manual respectively. Title pages will be prepared in manuscript.

Place	Date	Hour	Summary of Events and Information	Remarks and references to Appendices
HUBERSENT	17		Fine. Coy + Platoon Drill. Brigade Classes. Afternoon devoted to Bn. Range Sketches.	
	18		Route clear. Gas Drill. Bayonet fighting at H.Q.'s. TIMPRY.	
			Stormy. Short Parade divided. Conference for commanding officers of 49 Inf Bns troops. Coy Comds Conference at Bn. HQ.s. Bn Day of Rest. Orders for advance party received. Advance party officers & NCOs proceeded to 47 Inf (Int Hqrs). N.C.O.s were to employ party as instructed Runners.	
	19		Fine. Coy Drill. Bn Drill. Sections marched through & Inspected Huts. Recreational training. Divisions warned by wires. Rmv. to JULIEN.	
DIEVAL	20		Bn marched to HAUT TINGRY via SAMER - MONTREUIL Rd. entrained arrived at DIEVAL 6pm. Rest under cover for one night.	49 Inf Bde OO No. 10
NOEUX	21		Entrained 1pm & proceeded to NOEUX LES MINES; arrived 4pm, orders rec'd to relieve	
MINES			2 RRC Rt Coy 13th Bn Fusilier	49 Inf Bde O.O.
	22		Bn marched to the River LAMBRIN Sector.	
CAMBRIN	"		The Bn marched off from NOEUX LES MINES and relieved the 2 R.K.R.R.C. in the LAMBRIN Sector. Relief completed by 2.30pm. Quiet day. Casualties 1 other rank died of wounds. In costs Rest. One Artillery shelled AUCHY about 6pm.	

Army Form C. 2118.

WAR DIARY
or
INTELLIGENCE SUMMARY.
(Erase heading not required.)

Instructions regarding War Diaries and Intelligence Summaries are contained in F. S. Regs., Part II. and the Staff Manual respectively. Title pages will be prepared in manuscript.

Place	Date	Hour	Summary of Events and Information	Remarks and references to Appendices
CAMBRIN	Aug 23		Fine. Quiet night. Area A26 N.30.25. Artillerearth emerging gas about 1.15 am. 2 shells. Conference for Bn. Commanders at Bde. Bn. H.Qrs 10.30 am. Conferences for OC Coys at Bn. H.Qrs. 4.30 pm. Quiet seteum. Casualties nil	
	24		Dull, some rain. A quiet night. Bombardment on our life, N of LABASSÉE Canal 7.30 am. again about 9.45 am. E.A. flew low over our lines 7.20 am. 4 again 11.20 am. Rather quiet noticed at intervals during the day. 2 Lt A.E. Nightingale wounded, 1 other rank wounded.	
	25		Fine. A quiet night. Began fire at intervals. Our Patrol reached German 2nd line encoucied at the point reached. Red Station Bearer does daily under M.O. Artillery carries out harassing fire 9 am to 7.30 pm. Casualties Nil.	
	26		Wet. Quiet night. 1 Officer & 1 N.C.O. per Company reconnoitred CAMBRIN defences held by 3/4th London Regt. Orders received to relieve 3/4th London Regt. night of 27th. 1 Platoon to relieve New platoon in PONT FIXE Post on night of 27th. Normal day, enemy shelled CAMBRIN from 7.30 pm onwards. Casualties Nil. E.A. inactive.	47 E by Pt. Order No. 13
	27		Fine. 4 am Artillery bombardment on our life. Our Howitzer Batteries replied this morning. I sawed Lifen enemy book house on LABASSÉE - BOUVROY R. Enemy shells Bn. H.Qrs with 4.2 v Blue Cross Gas 10 pm - 12 midnight. No 6 platoon took over PONT FIXE 4.40 relieved by 6 pltn. 3/4th London Regt. Casualties Nil.	

(A7092) Wt W12859/M1893. 75,10. 6. 1/17. D. D. & L., Ltd. Forms/C.2118/14.

Army Form C. 2118.

WAR DIARY
or
INTELLIGENCE SUMMARY.
(Erase heading not required)

Instructions regarding War Diaries and Intelligence Summaries are contained in F. S. Regs., Part II. and the Staff Manual respectively. Title pages will be prepared in manuscript.

Place	Date	Hour	Summary of Events and Information	Remarks and references to Appendices
CAMBRIN	28		Enemy artillery more active. LANE & MILL TOWER Rds. shelled by 150 m.m. from 1 a.m. onwards. Relief complete 4.30 p.m. Bn. moved into Support at CAMBRIN, in billets. 5.30 p.m. Casualties 2 O.Rs. wounded.	
	29		Quiet night, fine. Working parties under R.E. 300 men 9 a.m. small parties at 1.30 p.m. 6 p.m. Parks at ANNEQUIN. 60 men parties 9-12 p.m. 2-5 p.m. Working parties for D.T.M.O. 2 A cnt at 7.30 a.m. 4-5.30 pm. Casualties 1 O.R. wd.(slight) 10 men carrying for D.T.M.O. Demonstration at Bde. H.Q.	
	30		Fine. Quiet night. Working parties as yesterday. Demonstration at Bde. H.Q. with contact aeroplane. Baths at ANNEQUIN as yesterday. Casualties NIL.	
	31		CAMBRIN shelled with Blue × at 10-15 pm. Dull. Working parties as yesterday. Demonstration at Bn. HQrs. to visit aeroplane Casualties NIL.	

Manningford
Capt. C. Commanding

6th Somerset Light Infantry.

VOLUME 40

WAR DIARY FOR

September 1918.

WAR DIARY or INTELLIGENCE SUMMARY.

Army Form C. 2118.

(Erase heading not required.)

Instructions regarding War Diaries and Intelligence Summaries are contained in F. S. Regs., Part II. and the Staff Manual respectively. Title pages will be prepared in manuscript.

Place	Date 1918 Sept.	Hour	Summary of Events and Information	Remarks and references to Appendices
CAMBRIN	1		Belt. Quiet night. E.A. flew over canal 6.30 a.m. Working parties under R.E. Interrupting received 10-10 p.m. enemy light. Raising front rising W. of AUCHY. Patrols going forward.	
	2	6.30 a.m.	Quiet night. E.A. over 6.30 a.m. Bn. No.1 received no enemy raiding. Normal. Sections relieved. Casualties NIL. Our artillery active 10.45 p.m. – 11.30 p.m.	
	3		Quiet night. Enemy artillery more to N. 4.30 a.m. E.A. over 1.20 p.m. 3 p.m. Ers. Engaged by AA on Bn. front 10 p.m. (a) NIL.	
	4	11.40 a.m. 12.50 p.m.	Fine. E.A. over at 11.40 a.m. 12.50 p.m. Enemy artillery active, firing on Nelson and of CAMBRIN. Conference re O.C. Battn. at Command Post CAMBRIN. Cas NIL.	
	5	6 a.m. 6.30 a.m. 9.15 a.m. 12.40 p.m.	Fine, quiet night. E.A. low over CAMBRIN at 6 a.m. 6.30 a.m. 9.15 a.m. 12.40 p.m. otherwise quiet. Casualties NIL.	
	6	1.30 a.m. to 2 a.m. 4.30 a.m. 5.30 p.m.	Fine. Orders received 1.30 a.m. to 2 a.m. 2 Coys. up to 2 North Eu. Reps to 3 Zouches Reps. up. Bde. by 4.30 a.m. so as a garrison, less battn. being ordered to attack at 5.30 p.m. Orders received to Saft-24. take over from 2 North Zue in Villages, afterwards relieved by 18th Glo Regt. CAMBRIN. Clos	
	7	10.15 p.m. 11.30 p.m. 12 noon.	Fine. Ordered to relieve 2nd London Regt. in trench line. Commence to Villages 12 noon. Commenced 10.15 p.m. No. 1 Cor. relief carried 11.30 p.m.	

WAR DIARY or INTELLIGENCE SUMMARY

Army Form C. 2118.

(Erase heading not required.)

Place	Date	Hour	Summary of Events and Information	Remarks and references to Appendices
CANBRAI	Sept 7		Orders received 18th Divn. to relieve 22 North Div. on night of 8/9. Relief complete 1.0 am.	44th Bde Order
	8 (Sun)	2.0 am	N.Y.D. Gas	No 22
			Dull, quiet night. Patrols noticed Rly. Cottage & N.Z. embankment held from R.R.	
(In the line)	9		Quiet day & night. R.R.Bn.	
		6.00	17.0G. N.Y.D. (gas)	
			Quiet night. Patrol sent out from RYAN ALLEY found no enemy but trench in a good state of repair. Our Artillery active 9 - 10.30 am. Orders received to take RAILWAY COTTAGE A.22.D.90.00. This was fastened by wire 9.45 pm. Cao 2 N.Y.D. (gas)	49th Bde Order 27
			(8/0) now wounded (gas)	D.G.S. N.Y.D. B.M. 146
	10		Wet. Patrol reconnoitered wire in front of Rly. Cottage, found a ladder, fell in one Sgt. Horn wired. Sermon in N.G. Post A.2.2.D.05.60. Two other patrols were out. RYANSALLEY Orders of the previous day to attack received. Enemy shelled Bn. HQrs. HARLEY STREET area	44th Bde Order 28
		5.0 pm	Cao 9030 reported N.Y.D. (800) Map wind Th. mist now confirmed N.Y.D. (gas).	
		20Rs	N.Y.D. (gas) 10R. Mustard	
	11		Quiet night. We attacked at 5-15 am. in accordance with orders, all objectives taken, 1 Heavy M.G. captured, 15 prisoners taken & 4 wounded prisoners taken. Enemy strength about 30. Counter-attacked our right boat, beaten off with heavy losses.	

WAR DIARY
or
INTELLIGENCE SUMMARY.

Army Form C. 2118.

Place	Date	Hour	Summary of Events and Information	Remarks and references to Appendices
(In Line) (cont)	11 Sept		Bttn on our left were counter attacked withdrew from SPOTTED DOG to Helen's FRANKS KEEP allowing the enemy to take us in to rear at Ply Cottage and bombed to SPOTTED DOG and salved a Lewis Gun left by Lge Bttn. Line then withdrawn to normal positions. Orders received 1.10pm to attack at 5.30pm to take RAILWAY COTTAGE Rly Embankment. Line with a barrage (about hundred of Piccadilly attack) Cas. 7/K 2/Lt Parsons wdd 30R killed 6.0R wdd 50R M.N. D(?) Bttn started at 5.45pm. Barrage opened at 5.30pm killing 5.45pm. All objectives taken - no opposition on path. Enemy ran away on life. Consolidated 7/Lt R.J. Botham wdd - v died of wounds. Capt E.H.C Cook wdd AT DUTY 30R Killed 1 OR killed (accidentally) 9 OR wounded	4/98 Rtn Batt 37
	12		Fairly quiet night. AUBURN Trench still heavily Sh. Bn HQ moved to Robertsons Tunnel. Orders received to be relieved by 24th London Regt. 39/12	BM order 30
		3am	Orders received to push patrols forward. Occupy the line West of AUCHY. Patrols Ken to build forward outpost established E of AUCHY. These were done at 5.30pm without opposition. 1 MG only firing. Enemy consolidation being at the approach	BM 239
AUCHY	13		Our troops AUCHY were roommates 43 posts established at 9.0pm B.25-90 and at without opposition. AUCHY shown by day	wk Sta order 31

A/23. C.9.8. Enemy (ills) AUCHY showing by day

WAR DIARY
or
INTELLIGENCE SUMMARY.

(Erase heading not required.)

Army Form C. 2118.

Place	Date	Hour	Summary of Events and Information	Remarks and references to Appendices
AUCHY	Sep 13 (cont)		Relief complete 6pm. Bn moved into Div. Reserve at CAMBRIN.	
CAMBRIN	14		Quiet night. Enemy shelled CAMBRIN at intervals and Shrapnel Cas NIL	
	15		Fine. Enemy shelled CAMBRIN at intervals during the day. Parades Square Baths. B.O. 37. L'gn g S Bearer Party. Cas NIL	
	16		Fine. Quiet night. Orders received Div on our left would attack x ravage CANTELEUX TRENCH	B.O. 34
			This cancelled by wire.	Order 19.
			Orders received to relieve the 20th London Regt in the line 17/18. Baths, Instructions	B.O. 35
			in throwing egg bombs. Notes 33 the Platoon in defence. Boy. Commanders	
			Conference 12 NOON. Capt E.H.C took proceeded on leave. BO received refer attack on	B.O. 36
CANTELEUX	17/9/18		Enemy. Sgt Kinnell Wnd (acc.ly)	
	17		Fine after a Hundredstorm during the night. 24h Coys relieved on the morning, Relief	
		12 NOON	complete 12 NOON, remainder of Bn. relieved at dusk complete 9.40 pm. Enemy amount	
			of Blue & Yellow Cross Gas shelling during the evening	
	18		Quiet night, fine day. E.A over our lines 12.40 pm. Enemy counts attacked Bn on our	
		1 pm	left. 1 pm Hook A17, D92.10. Enemy shelled AUCHY 7 - 7.45 pm. Cas NIL	
	19		Fine. Enemy shelled AUCHY "C" on work 7.7am. Very quiet day. (1 or Pl Eastwell wnd (accidly))	

Army Form C. 2118a

WAR DIARY
or
INTELLIGENCE SUMMARY.
(Erase heading not required.)

Instructions regarding War Diaries and Intelligence Summaries are contained in F. S. Regs., Part II. and the Staff Manual respectively. Title pages will be prepared in manuscript.

Place	Date	Hour	Summary of Events and Information	Remarks and references to Appendices
	1918 Sept.			
OMYBRIN	20		2 Brigades shelled 40 rounds 77 M.M. Yellow gas 6-7am	48 Bde
			Fine. Quiet 24 hours. Orders recvd to be relieved by 34th London Regt on 21st Cas. NIL.	Order 21
	21		Some storms. Quiet day. Relief complete 10.30pm. One of our aeroplanes fell in A24 a5.7 about 7pm. In support by 11pm Cas NIL. HQrs BRADDELL POINT.	Bde. Order 22
BRADDELL POINT.	22		Quiet night. 100 Blue + Yellow + gas shells village nr. 2 am. Orders recvd to relieve 34th London Regt night of 24/25th also orders of relief of 48th Fn. 13. Cas. NIL	Bde Order 24-25
	23		Fine. Quiet day, enemy shelled POINT de FIXE intermittently. Cas. NIL	
	24		Fine. Enemy shelled BRADDEL POINT 10 minutes 77 M.M. 3.45pm. 18 gun windiness received 34 London Regt in AUCHY Sector, relief complete 11.50 pm. Cas NIL	
AUCHY			Lieut R.W. BONIN admitted hospital	
	25		Fine but dull, quiet return, wind showing at moments to be enemy. Cas nil	
	26		Some storms. Enemy shelled AUCHY and our front line intermittently	B.O. 40
	27		Fine often wet night. Gas shelling LES BRIQUES + BROIS KEEP Cas nil during the day. Bn. relieved by 48 Inf Bn. Bn. reinforced by 5 hrs Bn. relief complete 11.15 pm. Bn. marched to DROUVIN CAMP, arrived in camp 3 am	
DROUVIN				

Army Form C. 2118.

WAR DIARY
or
INTELLIGENCE SUMMARY.
(Erase heading not required.)

Instructions regarding War Diaries and Intelligence Summaries are contained in F.S. Regs., Part II. and the Staff Manual respectively. Title pages will be prepared in manuscript.

Place	Date	Hour	Summary of Events and Information	Remarks and references to Appendices
DROUVIN	Sep 28		Fine. Cleaning up. Inspection Draft of 52 O.R's (31 cavalry) arrived	
	29		Showers. Baths. Inspection of kits	
	30		Gas Drill. Corps parade. Musketry pt. Drill. L.G. Bombing and Lewis gun class	

D. Drewpto
Capt. and Adjt. for
O.C. 6 Somerset L.I.

VOLUME 40.

WAR DIARY.
6th Service Battalion Somerset Light Infantry.

for the month

of

OCTOBER 1918.

Army Form C. 2118.

WAR DIARY
or
INTELLIGENCE SUMMARY.
(Erase heading not required.)

Instructions regarding War Diaries and Intelligence Summaries are contained in F. S. Regs., Part II. and the Staff Manual respectively. Title pages will be prepared in manuscript.

Place	Date	Hour	Summary of Events and Information	Remarks and references to Appendices
DROUVIN	1918 Oct 1		Fine. MINX Range. Parade under Coys. Lecture Trg. Classes. Lg. Bombing. Officers Lecture. PT under CSM Hobson AGS.	
	2		Fine. HESDIGNEUL Range. Daylight patrols, rapid wiring. Classes as previous day. Wiring returned the Refresher course at 3 hours notice	Bo 41 BM 461
	3		Order rec'd to move to SAILLY-LA-BOURSE. Bn to proceed by 7.30am	16 Div GHQ
SAILLY LA BOURSE			Bn marched to SAILLY LA BOURSE. Arrived in billets 12 noon	BM 363
	4		Fine. Coy training attend by trench wiring. 2" in command inspected Bn Hqts personnel. Bde/os officer inspected SBR's & Lewis Gun Hqts/Bn Hqts. Classes	
	5		Fine. Wiring at South. Bde/as officer inspected SBR's & Gas alarms under of the Battalion. Lg. PT. MGCo. Classes.	
	6		Dull. Bde Parade Service. Dispersion. Reconnoitring of forward areas by C.O., 2/c, Lewis gun officer. Conference at 49 Bde Hqts for Battn. Commanders	
	7		Fine. Platoon Training. Lewis Gun classes, S.B., bugler & Lg Courses. Conference at 49 Bde Hqts 12 noon Schem'n Lawrence Scheme.	Bo 41 Bo 42/1
NOEUX LES MINES	8		Bn marched to NOEUX LES MINES. Arrived in camp 12 noon	Bo 43
	9		Parade under Coy. Classes. Bombing, SB, PT, Lg, on miniature Range. Reconstituted Training.	

Army Form C. 2118.

WAR DIARY
or
INTELLIGENCE SUMMARY.
(Erase heading not required.)

Instructions regarding War Diaries and Intelligence Summaries are contained in F. S. Regs., Part II. and the Staff Manual respectively. Title pages will be prepared in manuscript.

Place	Date	Hour	Summary of Events and Information	Remarks and references to Appendices
NOEUX LES MINES	17		Bn moved to NOE to CAMBRIN. Detach Sn Ref Coy & 12 Offrs & 325 OR ranks attached to this Bath for the move. Bn marched Off 1315' to billets CAMBRIN 1600	B.m.u. 47
CAMBRIN	18		Bn moved to BERCLAU arrived in billets 1130 am. Bn marched Off at 16 billets	B.m.u. 48
BERCLAU				u.b
AUCHEL IN	19		AUCHEL IN arrived here 1700	48
PONT A MARCQ	20		Bn marched to PONT A MARCQ arrived in billets 1500	49
BACHY			Bn marched LES ESCOBURE arrived here 1500 rested met & marched to BACHY	
			Brassarie in billets 1930.	BM 357
RUMES	21		Bn marched to RUMES arrived 1130. Transport arrived 1500	So 996
	22		Bn resting. Co & Coy Comdrs reconnoitring forward areas	
	23		Bn working party 20 offrs 100 O ranks under 1/S Coy R.E. Impressions Inspection reconnaissance forward areas.	
	24		Still Working parties under 1S Coy R.E. 2 Offrs & 200 OR. General cleaning of fouling returns met to assure interior Regt in best free since 9.25. Bivouac party moved up 1700 tonight	B.q 52
ÉPINOY	25		Bn proceed to Line. Transport to FLORENT Bn marched to the line. Relief Complete 0300. 26/10/18	Bo 52

WAR DIARY or INTELLIGENCE SUMMARY

Army Form C. 2118.

Place	Date	Hour	Summary of Events and Information	Remarks and references to Appendices
On the line	Oct 26		Fine. Enemy Artillery & M.G. very active all night & again 1250 to 1350. M.G. shelling 0530 at V.17.B.6.2. One of our aeroplanes No.F900 crashed in front of our lines 1120. Body of Lt. R.F.G. Hinchon recovered. Cas. 1 O.R. wounded.	
	27		Fine. Quieter night early. Enemy attempted a raid upon one of our posts at V.20.A.O.B. Ration off M.G. rifle fire. 2 German killed, 1 Officer wounded, recovered, identification established 29 Regt. 5 other German wounded but got back to their own lines. At E.A.0. our own lines 0800 Enemy M.G. active before dawn. Bn. H.Q. Coy. shelled 1100–1500. 1 direct hit obtained. Cas. 3 O.R. wounded.	
	28		Wire Company ready and took their reliefs 2239. Relief reported Bn. to be relieved by 1/8/29 Fine. Enemy gas shells to whole area 0400. Blue & Enzyhemal E.A. actively shelled Ca & I.O.R. wounded 1 O.R. killed. Threat daily shelling of Bn. HQ 1400. Cas. Relief complete 2200. Road mend.	Do 54
TACTIGNIES	29		Fine. General cleaning up. Sig Amn. Fires by 77 cm Cas. 10 wounded	
	30		Fine. Parade under Coy arrangement. Working (in class Cuerneries) Bath on Reserve Line Trenches. Coy call.	
	31		Fine. Parade under or Corp. H & Coy. Overflow clothing took an Inactive Reserve line. Bath House during the night.	

31.10.18

R. Sharp Moor
Capt. and 6 Jan L!

43.N.
19 sheets

Confidential.

War Diary

6th. Bn. Somerset. L.I.

for

November 1918

Volume No. 41.

WAR DIARY
or
INTELLIGENCE SUMMARY.
(Erase heading not required)

Army Form C. 2118

46

Place	Date	Hour	Summary of Events and Information	Remarks and references to Appendices
WARGNIES	1918 1/Nov		Dull. Enemy harassing fire on front area. Working parties at Corps Rd class.	B.O. 63
	2		Fine. Enemy shell fire in rear areas to harass our troops during relief. Working parties during the night in forward areas. Parades in order as Corps. W.O. Rostes.	
	3		Wet. Working parties (6 platoons of 20 men each) in forward area during Eman: P.O.W. Platooned at Ruhn's area made to ??/fugal. Church Parade	B.O. 65
	4		Fine. Three companies on working parties in forward areas. Battalion relieves the 11th Yorks & Lancs in support of positions. Relief complete 18.30	
	5		Wet. Two companies working parties formed area. Cascalias L OR	
	6		Wet. Battalion relieved by 22nd Northumbrian Fusiliers and proceeded to RUMES in support group on completion of relief, Battalion at the entrance of B.F.G. 42 and proceed in view of sudden event. Relief complete 20.30. Trench rifts 2 BLS. Blanket drawn from Divisional store. Casualties 1 officer 30 OR.	B.O. 57
RUMES	7		Fine. General cleaning up. Casualties nil.	
	8		Wet. Enemy retired. E of ?? Brussels. Battalion standing by to move up if fortune	
	9		vacated by 4 A.F.Bgde. Bruxelles mit	
	10		Fine. Battalion under the Bye & Dun for Class Casualties nil	
BRUXELLES	11		Fine. Battalion moved up to BRUXELLES. Tr rifts 13.45. Casualties mil	B.O. 59
			Fine. Hostilities ceased at 11	
		10 a.m	Fine. Battalion "standing by" in field. Joint Parade Service with K.R.R.C. at	
	13		Fine. Parades under O.C. Coys.	
	14		Fine. Battalion paraded for P.O.C. Parade	
RUMES	15		Fine. Battalion marched to RUMES. Tr rifts 12.00	B.O. 62

Army Form C. 2118.

WAR DIARY
or
INTELLIGENCE SUMMARY.
(Erase heading not required.)

Instructions regarding War Diaries and Intelligence Summaries are contained in F. S. Regs., Part II. and the Staff Manual respectively. Title pages will be prepared in manuscript.

Place	Date 1918	Hour	Summary of Events and Information	Remarks and references to Appendices
BERSEE	Nov 16		Bns Batln. march to BERSEE – 12 miles – 3rd men fell out. Arr billets 18.30	R.O. 61
"	17		Sun. Rest. Day. Voluntary Church Service and baths	
"	18		Gen. Asst. Inst. Parades under ot. Coy. and recruitmental training. Butts	
"	19		Parades under the Companies. Army Educational classes started	
"	20		Parades under the Coy^s	
"	21		Parades under ot. Coy^s. 2nd round of figures in loss of equipment by fire in billet of No 8 Coy.	
"	22		Parades under ot. Companies	
"	23		Drafts. Commmrd Parade at 10.30 other Parades under ot. Coys.	
"	24		Church Parade. Gunnrt Officers and ot. Premier Catholic & Protestant Divine Service	
"	25		attended by [?] Church. Draft of 2 hundred OR. anns and systematic Salvage commenced	
"	26		All companies on Salvage. Batts. ordrs received that the Brigade would move	
"	27		Bns. Parades under ot. Batt^s. Batts.	
"	28		Cont. Parades under the Coy. Rovers and their carpenters making table [?] for	
"			Educ. Instr. During the day an Inspection [?] of walks and Rooms [?] by the CO	
"	29		Gen. Parade under ot. Coys. march out. Bgde.	
"	30		Parade under ot. Coys. march out. Bgde.	

R Brown Shee
Capt. on 6 Forward W

Vol 47

H.H.V.
3 sheets

Confidential.

War Diary.

for

December 1918

Volume No. 42

6th Bn. Somerset L.I.

WAR DIARY
or
INTELLIGENCE SUMMARY.
(Erase heading not required.)

Army Form C. 2118.

Instructions regarding War Diaries and Intelligence Summaries are contained in F.S. Regs., Part II. and the Staff Manual respectively. Title pages will be prepared in manuscript.

Place	Date 1918	Hour	Summary of Events and Information	Remarks and references to Appendices
BERSÉE	1		Fine and cold. Church Parade. 8 p.m. at Phelerin. Battalion defeated Holm at football and Duff Bow in Brigade competition	
	2		Fine. Battalion Ceremonial Parade	
	3		Wet. Company Parades and of Education	
	4		Wet. Do. Divisional Bands arrived	
				Boys Ground Conference 11:00
	5		Ceremonial guard mounting parade in the Square BERSÉE jointly with 17 Londons. 16th Div Band in attendance. Band circuit in streets 17:30	
	6		Fine. Brigade ceremonial parade in Hirge Form. BERSÉE Brigade Cross Country Run.	
	7		Fine. Parade under O.C. Boy and Education classes. 16th Div Band played in Square BERSÉE	
	8		Fine. Interior Economy and Parades under O.C. Coys. Div Band left	
	9		Fine. Church Parade	
	10		Wet. Battalion Route March	
	11		Wet. Parades under O.C. Boys Education	
	12		Wet. Do. 1 Corp Rata Meeting Manes Demobilisation commenced	
	13		Wet. Parades under O.C. Boys Education	
	14		Fine. Do. do Schools	
	15		Fine. Do. do Education	
	16		Fine. Street Parade	
	17		Wet. Battalion Route March Football. Battalion came to conclusion	
	18		Fine. Brigade under Hist Boy Education. Div Sports reported 10-1	
	19		Fine. Do. Parade under O.C. Coys Education	
	20		Fine. Do. do. units match	
	21		Fine. Do. do. do	
	22		Fine. Do. do. Brigade football team beat one panels beyond final. Div Final.	

WAR DIARY
or
INTELLIGENCE SUMMARY.

Army Form C. 2118.

Place	Date	Hour	Summary of Events and Information	Remarks and references to Appendices
BERSEE	Dec 23		Battalion General Parade	
	24		Parades under Coys Parades	
	25		Christmas Day	
	26		Parades under Coys Arrangements	
	27		do Battalion Parade march through village and rajos	
	28		do Gunnery and Education	
	29		do Church Parade	
	30		do Parades under Coys. Distribution of prizes at Regimental	
	31		do Parades under Coys Relaxation	

J. Crompton
Lt Col

VOLUME 43

WAR DIARY

6th Battalion Somerset Light Infantry.

JANUARY 1919.

Army Form C. 2118.

WAR DIARY
or
INTELLIGENCE SUMMARY.
(Erase heading not required.)

Instructions regarding War Diaries and Intelligence Summaries are contained in F.S. Regs., Part II. and the Staff Manual respectively. Title pages will be prepared in manuscript.

Place	Date 1919	Hour	Summary of Events and Information	Remarks and references to Appendices
BERSEE	Jan 1		Short Route March. Parades under Offr. Corps Education	
	2		Parades under Offr. Corps Education	
	3		Brigade Route March	
	4		Steeple Ceremony. Batt. visited loom but to D.O.C. in Divisional competition	
	5		Church Parade	
	6		Battalion Route March	
	7		Parades under Offr. Corps. Sent of Engineer as to defence of Mobile Equipment	
	8		Draft of 10 for demobilisation. Parades under Offr. Corps Education	
	9		Parades under Offr. Corps Education	
	10		Battalion on Labour in humour.	
	11		Parades under Offr. Corps Education	
	12		Church Parade	
	13		Battalion on Labour in area and draft of 30 men for demobilisation.	
	14		Companies on parade under Offr. Corps Education. Burning Guard mounted at Divisional Pond	
	15		Parades under Offr. Corps Education	
	16		Parades under Offr. Corps. Education. Transport Competition won by Ration	
	17		Battalion Route March. Education	
	18		Parades under Offr. Corps. Education	
	19		Church Parade	

Army Form C. 2118.

WAR DIARY
or
INTELLIGENCE SUMMARY.
(Erase heading not required.)

Instructions regarding War Diaries and Intelligence Summaries are contained in F. S. Regs., Part II. and the Staff Manual respectively. Title pages will be prepared in manuscript.

Place	Date 1919	Hour	Summary of Events and Information	Remarks and references to Appendices
BERSÉE	Jan 20		Battalion Route March. Party of 5 men despatched for demobilisation	
	21		Fine. Parades under Coy. Comds. Lecture by Mr. J.W. Fell on "Sport".	
	22		Battalion parade. Adj. Board.	
	23		Fine. Parades under Coy. Comds. Boys & Baths. Divisional Football final at Romer won by "Lahore".	
	24		Coy parade. Route march.	
	25		Suit. Parades under Coys.	
	26		Snow. Church Parades. Battalion wore the Divisional Day of Man.	
	27		Battalion Route march. Party of 61 men despatched for demobilisation	
	28		Snow. Parades under Coys.	
	29		Snow. Parades under Coys. Capt. Education	
	30		Frost. Parades wore of Capt. Education. Baths	
	31		Snow. Parade under Capt. Education	

N. Hawkstone
Capt. D.y.
for Commdg. 5/

VOLUME 44.
WAR DIARY for Month of
FEBRUARY, 1919.
6th BATTALION SOMERSET LIGHT INFANTRY.
B E F.

WAR DIARY
or
INTELLIGENCE SUMMARY.
(Erase heading not required.)

Army Form C. 2118.

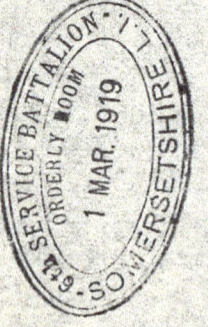

Place	Date	Hour	Summary of Events and Information	Remarks and references to Appendices
BERSEE	1919 Feb 1		Parades under O/C Coys	
	2		Church Parade attended by N/R.M. the Prince of Wales.	
	3		Education Parade under O/C Coy	
	4		Bttn Ceremonial Parade Rehearsal for forthcoming ceremony.	
	5		Parades under O/C Coys. Education. Baths.	
	6		Parades under O/C Coys.	
	7		Bttn Ceremonial Parade, Private ___ Attg VC Colour bearer Ceremony	
	8		Parades & Games under O/C Coys. Education	
	9		Church Parade.	
	10		Baths. Route March	
	11		Parades under O/C Coys. O/C Coys Education	
	12		The Leave Bus under O/C Coys. Education	
	13		Parades under O/C Coys. P.T. + S. + Education	
	14		10 O/C Coys. Games	
	15		Conveyance of 9 Coys. Three for Army of Occupation to form one Coy. Major ___	
			remained in Bttn. Added to Bttn. Wire sides & dep. Coys, Major ___	
	16		Church Parade for Cadre Remainder by 10/9 by middle of week (22)	
	17		Parade under O/C Coy. (Brest up before)	
	18		Parade under O/C Coy.	
	19		Parade under O/C Coys. Cadre of classes at Bray Village	
	20		Parade under O/C Coys.	
	21		also under O/C Coys.	
	22		Parades under O/C Coys.	

Army Form C. 2118.

WAR DIARY
or
INTELLIGENCE SUMMARY.
(Erase heading not required.)

Instructions regarding War Diaries and Intelligence Summaries are contained in F. S. Regs., Part II. and the Staff Manual respectively. Title pages will be prepared in manuscript.

[Stamp: 6. SERVICE BATTALION S.L.I. SOMERSETSHIRE ORDERLY ROOM 1 MAR. 1919]

Place	Date	Hour	Summary of Events and Information	Remarks and references to Appendices
BERSEE	1919 Feb 23		Church Parade for Cadre + demobilisation lays.	
	24		Sup (A) conducting 7 2 Officers + 180 O.R.s who proceeded to 11th Bn. L.I.	
			3rd Army 2 respectively. Balance employed to take up duties of General Fatigues, also as far as men ask not at present suitable for release.	
	25			
	26		Personnel employed as above.	
	27			
	28			

1/3/19

G.W.Hope
Capt Ayr.
6th Bn Somerset L.I.

WAR DIARY

VOLUME 45

of

6th Service Battalion Somerset Light Infantry

for

the month of

MARCH 1919.

Army Form C. 2118.

WAR DIARY
or
INTELLIGENCE SUMMARY.
(Erase heading not required.)

Instructions regarding War Diaries and Intelligence Summaries are contained in F. S. Regs., Part II. and the Staff Manual respectively. Title pages will be prepared in manuscript.

Place	Date	Hour	Summary of Events and Information	Remarks and references to Appendices
Bernes	March 1			
	2			
	3/8			
	9			
	10			
	11			
	15/15		3 Officers posted to Pay M Coys. Strength 27 Officers 108 O.R's	
	16		Parade & Address men O.C. Coy. Church Parade.	
	17/22		Parade. Strength mill O.C. Coy	
	23		Church Parade.	
	24/25		Inspection by C.O. Strength 17 Officers 98 O.R's	
	26/29		Parade. Strength mill O.C. Coy.	

Army Form C. 2118.

WAR DIARY
or
INTELLIGENCE SUMMARY.
(Erase heading not required.)

Instructions regarding War Diaries and Intelligence Summaries are contained in F. S. Regs., Part II. and the Staff Manual respectively. Title pages will be prepared in manuscript.

Place	Date	Hour	Summary of Events and Information	Remarks and references to Appendices
Bence	March 30		Strength 10 Officers 97 ORs Church Parade Parade taken under O.C.Y.	
	31			

G.C. Hodge
Capt. & Adjutant.
6th Somerset Light Infantry

WAR DIARY

for

Month of APRIL 1919.

Volume No 46.

6th Service Battalion Somerset Light Infantry.

WAR DIARY
or
INTELLIGENCE SUMMARY.

(Erase heading not required.)

Army Form C. 2118.

Place	Date	Hour	Summary of Events and Information	Remarks and references to Appendices
Birci Bqt France	1/4/19 to 30/4/19		Guards & Fatigues	

G.B. Copey
Capt & Adjt
6th Service Battalion Bornard R.

www.ingramcontent.com/pod-product-compliance
Lightning Source LLC
Chambersburg PA
CBHW081459160426
43193CB00013B/2533